This is something about self-expression.

OTHER BOOKS BY ROBERT M. DRAKE

Spaceship (2012)

Science (2013)

Beautiful Chaos (2014)

Black Butterfly (2015)

A Brilliant Madness (2015)

Beautiful and Damned (2016)

Broken Flowers (2016)

Seed Of Chaos (2017)

Gravity: A Novel (2017)

Moon Theory (2017)

Young & Rebellious (2018)

Chasing The Gloom (2018)

Samuel White & The Frog King (2018)

For Excerpts and Updates please follow:

Instagram.com/rmdrk
Facebook.com/rmdrk
Twitter.com/rmdrk

ISBN: 978-0-9986293-3-9

Book Cover: Robert M. Drake
Cover Image licensed by Shutter Stock Inc.

For Sevyn,

All my words are yours.
All of my words, will always be yours.

CONTENTS

STAR THEORY

ROBERT M. DRAKE

MUST HAPPEN

That's the problem.

There are certain things
you can't change,
things that must happen.

Like who you meet and why.
Where you go
and how long it takes you
to get there.

Bad or good.
Rain or shine.

Whatever happens, happens.

But you could change something.

You could change your outlook—
how things affect you—
how they move you
and how they make you feel.

So yes,
sadness is sadness,
broken is broken.

There's no lie in that

but you have a heart
and it adapts to change.

It picks itself up,
keeps you alive and keeps going,
and *that's what counts*.

The way things change around you,
the way things break you,
and still,
you have it in you to take life head on
and with a smile.

You take change
and make it look beautiful.

You grow into a better person
no matter how many turns
your path gives you.

WHO FALLS

You can't control
who falls in love with whom.

Although,
at first,
it may seem as if you can,
but you can't.

People fall in love unexpectedly,
with the most unexpected people.

And no one ever sees it coming.

And when it does,
most of the time,
it's over right before it begins,
or so it seems.

Then,
you look back
and wonder how it happened.

You try to puzzle the pieces:
every moment, every exchange.

You try to pinpoint everything,
to recreate the same kind of love,
but it doesn't happen.

You can't find your soul mate
in other people's eyes.

You can't go around thinking
you're going to recreate
the same magic.

Like I said,
people fall in love at the most random
of times,
and you could never have
the same love twice.

Not today or tomorrow.

There's only one person
your heart belongs to
and it's usually the one who breaks it,

unexpectedly,
at any given time.

WHAT GROWS

Sadness grows.

Hearts shatter.

Love fades.

Time goes on...

and that doesn't change
for anybody.

WHERE IT BEGAN

I know how hard it is to move on,
especially
when it is all you've known.

I know pain means you care
and I know caring means
holding on.

I know the cycle,
that is,
you forgive to find yourself back
where you started.

I know you think you're weak,
that giving chances
makes you vulnerable.

I know some nights you find yourself
reminiscing of the good times—
before your sun was devoured
by sadness, by darkness.

I know it's hard to let go
when you know
they are no good to you.

And I know something inside of you
keeps telling you to hold on…

but don't feel too bad
for feeling the way you do—
for wanting more—a way out.

People consist of coming
and going.

They are made of memories
and dreams.

So moving on shouldn't be
such a terrible thing,
and letting go of people who don't care
shouldn't be so hard.

So move on,
but do it for yourself
and no one else.

Do it because it is
the right thing to do.

Do it to heal.

Do it to prove to yourself
that you're worth saving.

Do it because you should
love yourself
more than anyone else
and lastly,

do it because deep down inside of you,

you know
you deserve more.

FEELINGS ON

You can't turn off feelings.
Your heart is not a machine.

And you can't just turn them on
when needed
and off when not.

And you can't tell it what to feel
or when to feel.

That kind of thing happens on its own
because it's alive,
despite what you've read in books.

Your heart has a mind of its own,
and sometimes
you're not going to agree with it.

Sometimes, you're going to fight it
until one of you
surrenders.

So pay attention,
because *this is important*.

One day,
your heart is going to connect
with someone,

and it might be the right
or wrong person.

And you will feel things
you've probably never felt before
and things will either go to shit
or bloom in a garden of dreams.

But soon enough
it finds its end.

Love finds its end
and what you feel might remain…

because when you've built trust
with someone
that kind of connection never goes away,

It stays with you.
It dies with you.
It never learns to drift.

It becomes you…

whether that person stays

with you
or not.

UGLY TRUTH

If someone ever tells you
they didn't care,
that's a lie
because everyone cares
to some degree.

Because when it comes down to it,
it's about what they want
and what they do
to get it.

Who they want
and what they tell them
to get them within their grasp.

So maybe you fell in love
and they didn't.
That's okay,
but it doesn't mean they didn't care.

It just means their way of caring
was different from yours
because you can't expect people
to see things the way you do.

You can't expect them
to feel and think
the same way either.

If they want to spend time with you,
they care.

If they call you,
think of you,
write to you.

They care
regardless of what happens.

It's just some people have
a different way of showing it.

That's all.

TOO MUCH DIRT

You are never done
with feeling too much.

Your heart doesn't shut
itself off,
and you can't ignore
the possibility.

For example,
lovers are going to get hurt
the most.
That's the way it happens.

They feel more,
forgive more
and that doesn't make them weak.

It makes them strong
for giving people chances,
for putting others before themselves,

And that takes guts.

That takes true strength.

To feel what others feel,
to help them

and

never ask for anything
in return.

ONE DAY AGAIN

Because one day,
you're going to stop
putting yourself down.

One day,
you're going to grab a mirror
and look yourself in the eyes
and know that you're enough.

You're going to see yourself,
your true self,
for the very first time
and smile.

You're going to remember
all of those moments
when you hated yourself the most,
and you're going to know the difference
between who you are
and who they told you to be.

One day,
I promise you,
you will change.

Your life will change

and you will love it

for what it is.

And you will find peace
in the burning of the past
and you will never look back.

Nothing will ever be the same.

Your life will finally
be *your life*.

I promise you.

You owe it to yourself.

EMPTINESS IN

I feel things
but my heart is empty.

The same way
I want to love you
but there is not
a thing
left of me
to give.

MOST PEOPLE

I assume
most people only
find love the moment
they lose it

and

pass through their lives
chasing the people
who were never meant
to be theirs
at all.

INTENSITY

Sometimes
you're going to love
the wrong person,

and sometimes
you're going to get hurt
in the process.

Not everyone is going to care
and love
with the same intensity.

Not everyone *knows*
how to place the people they need
before others.

People take people
for granted every day,

despite how long
they've been with them,
what they've done for them, etc.

So you shouldn't change
what your heart feels
because of that.

You shouldn't let

a few lost people
direct your path.

Because you love
and you do so,
so effortlessly,
and that's a blessing.

That's the kind of gift
you want to give
to others…

whether people notice

or not.

SAME POEM OVER & OVER

Lovers are going to get hurt
the most.
That's the way it happens.

They feel more,
forgive more
and that doesn't make them weak.

It makes them strong.
It makes them brave.

It makes them more than human.

Because they give people chances
no matter what happens.

They carry hope with them
no matter how bad it hurts,
and that type of thing takes guts.

And I see that in you.

You're a lover
and with an open heart
you feel what others feel.

You want to help them
and fight for them.

You want to save
everyone you love
without asking for anything
in return.

And I know you'll do it regardless,
whether it breaks you

or not.

RISKY BUSINESS

You don't need to explain anything.

I know letting people in
is a risky business.

I know the pros
and cons of love.

Everyone does
but does that mean
we have to follow the rules?

Most likely not, right?

No one enters a relationship
with a contract—one that states
that if you destroy them
you'd have to pay for the damages.

No, no, and for god's sake, *no*.

It doesn't happen like that.
(Although some of us wish it did.)

So you don't need to explain
why you must go
because I knew this would happen.

Shit,

lately everyone,
one way or another
has been leaving me behind,
and it's been everyone
I've let in.

I'm beginning to think
I'm THAT fucked up,
that I'm too much for my own good.

So go
or better yet, I'll go.

I'll make it easier for you
because I probably
would have done the same.

I would have loved you,
convinced you of
how we are meant to be together forever
to suddenly realize
how it was all a mistake.

How it was all a fling.

Love is like that.

Sometimes it makes you believe
in something that's not really there.

And sometimes,
you believe in it a little too much,
so much
that it makes you blind
to the harsh realities.

Letting people in
is a risky business
but indeed,

there is nothing riskier
than falling in love.

SOMETHING CRAZY

People are afraid
of losing the people
they love—
the people they need.

Therefore,
if needed,
they'll do something out of the ordinary.

Something crazy,
you know?

And it doesn't matter
how or what?

They'll do anything to salvage
whatever is left
of the relationship.

They'll even betray their own thoughts
and logic.

People get desperate,
you know?

Love does that to you.

It can change you

from one day to the next.

It can bring you closer to the light
or leave you stranded in darkness.

Hell,
love is the last gasp before free diving
into the ocean,

and people,
well,

people will always be too afraid
that perhaps,
they didn't breathe in

enough air.

THE CHASE

I'm tired of chasing after people.

I'm tired to fighting for them,
and I'm tired of saving them.

I'm tired of putting my time
and effort in people
who don't care—
people whose words
don't match their actions.

I'm tired,
exhausted,
of giving too much,
of receiving too little.

And I know you can't understand this
because you're on the other side
of the situation.

I chase you.
I rescue you.
I care for you
and do things

for you

to make your life easier

but who's there for me?

Who's there to comfort me
when I feel as if
I don't have enough in me?

When I don't want to keep going?

See,
the problem is,
I've given you more
than I should have
and that has made you blind.

And I say this
because you think
I won't leave.

You think
I don't have the guts
to do so
but you're wrong.

You're wrong about everything.

DEAD WRONG!

I love myself
and the only regret I have is
that I didn't realize this sooner.

Only I can save myself
and I don't need a pair
of weak hands

to try and save me
as I fall.

NO PRAYERS

You shouldn't look for answers
in the people who left you.

There are no revelations there.
No guides.

No fulfillments of any kind.

You're not going to find a map
to paradise in these people.

You're going to find confusion,
and a lot more questions,
perhaps even more
than you can handle.

And I know people change,
that is,
if they want to
but why give in?

Why trust someone
who has broken you before
to begin with?

I mean,
people leave
and sometimes they have the nerve

to come back.

They forget what they've done
and act like everything
is well,
but that doesn't mean
you've got to let them back in.

You don't have to.

You owe it to yourself
to be happy—to be good.

Besides,
look at you now.

You're a goddamn superstar
and in their absence
you found more.
You found yourself

and your smile.

You found your inspiration,
your laughter
and all things that spark your senses.

You're stronger,
wiser and to be honest,

you don't need to spiral

around the bullshit
their universe brings.

You don't need the people
who have hurt you
to try and convince you
of how beautiful
you are.

You're a flower
and you don't drown
the moment the rain
starts falling down.

THE IRONY

It's ironic, you know?
Being alone,
not having anyone
to go home to
because it never really works
in your favor.

For example,
when you're alone,
most of the time you're missing someone.

You're full of ache
and wonder
and when you're with someone,
it doesn't matter who it is.

You find yourself zoning out,
far beyond anyone's reach.

Ironic enough,
it is the same way
with almost everything.

When you want
you don't have,
and when you have
you ignore what you have
'til it's gone.

And when it's gone,
you wish it was still here.

And it's the same with people
and love.

When you're ready to love,
they're not.

And when they're ready,
you've already moved on.

The irony, you know?

To always find yourself,
your TRUE self and love
in the wrong place
and at the wrong time.

FORGOTTEN ONES

I think you've forgotten
how hope could be found
in all places.

So don't tell me
you've given up.

Every day
is a new day

and each day
you have a second chance.

But I could see why
you feel like this

because most people
don't think this way.

Most people
fail
and believe it's okay to stop
what they love,

to put their dreams
on hold.

But you're not like most people.

In fact,
you're not like anyone
I've ever met at all.

You're different
and I don't mean

"you're different"

because not everyone
is the same.

What I mean is
you see the world differently.

The way you express yourself
so eloquently…

I've never witnessed anything
like that before.

You carry love,
real love
and spread it around
because you genuinely care.

So this is me
giving some of that back,

because as your friend,
I, too,

genuinely care.
And it's my duty to tell you that
you'll have better days tomorrow.

That

you've got to hang in there
no matter what.

Pain fades, my sweet friend,
but hope
and love

will always remain.

THINK YOU ARE NOT

How could you think
you're weak,
when every time you fall
you come back stronger
than before.

How could you think
you're not enough,
when every night
you discover you are
a little more.

How could you think
you're not special,
when every time you create something
it touches strangers
in ways they could have never
imagined.

How could you think
you're not loved,
when there are so many people
who need you,
who call out for you
when you're not around.

So tell me
why you doubt yourself.

Tell me what
is holding you back
from being who you want to become.

Is it fear?

Is it self-doubt?

Is it the feeling
of people
expecting too much from you?

I know what that's like.
I know what it's like to carry
a dream,
to carry a love,
perhaps,
even too big
for your own heart.

I know what it's like
to not have enough words
to tell the people you care about
how much they mean
to you.

All these things
can leave you submerged.

They can really turn
day into night.

So please,
don't be so hard on yourself.

Self-doubt is a slow killer
but there is nothing deadlier

than not believing
in yourself.

IT IS HARD, MAN

You can't just come
into people's lives
and expect them
to stop everything for you.

You can't just change
someone's life
because you have feelings for them.

You can't force people to love you,
to make them stay.

That's the type of thing
that makes them
turn around, you know?

And it's funny,
how hard it gets
as time goes on.

The more you lose,
the more you want to hold on,
but that's the irony of it all,
of life, right?

That's why it's hard
to keep a balance between
what you need

and what you want.

Between what hurts
and what heals.

And it's difficult to make people
understand
because most of them
are too busy
trying to solve their own problems.

So you can't expect people
to let you in right away.

You've got to earn
what you deserve
and you've got to know it
when you see it,

otherwise

you might lose it
forever.

Chance encounters
happen every day,
but second chances
are hard to come by.

You've got to find
who you need

and stay,
but only

if they want you to.

RIGHT PEOPLE

The right people
find you when you need them
to find you.

So I wouldn't worry
too much
about being alone,
and I wouldn't worry
too much
about being with someone
either.

Because right now,
you're where you have to be,
regardless of how you feel,
regardless of what you want.

Right now,
your life is preparing you
for something better,
for someone *worth it*.

And I know you complain about it.

I know you think
there's no one out there
for you,
but you're wrong,

goddamn it!

There is
and perhaps,
that person is probably feeling
the same way you are feeling.

Hell, perhaps,
they're waiting for that perfect moment
to bump into someone…

the same way you are.

Breathe it all in.

And that's how it happens,
as if it's some kind of miracle.

Some chance encounter,
some rare luck
that only happens once
in a lifetime,
but it's not.

It's just you,
meeting the love of your life
for the first time.

The way it was written
in the stars.
Like I said,

the right people
will always find you
at the right time.

All you have to do
is wait.

Love makes no mistakes
no errors
no runarounds,

and people could either be

a blessing or a lesson.

You decide.

SOUL IN THE EYES

And as time went on,
she carried this
unfiltered sadness
in her eyes.

And still,
she had the courage
to start anew.

To love again.

To be strong
enough to push the world
off its axis.

To be honest,
I don't know what it was.

Maybe it was her past.
Maybe it was her
uncertain future
that gave her something
to believe in again.

Nonetheless,
it was inspiring.

To know

that she could overcome things.

To rise.
Torealize
that she *did* matter.

You see,
now when I think of her…
write about her…

It's liberating.

It sets my soul free,
even if it is only
for a little while.

She makes me want to lose myself
to find myself
completely and unexpectedly.

She gives me life,
this unforgotten woman,

and I give her my time,

and together I create moments
worth remembering.

Too bad she is no longer
with us, with me.

She is just another story
and I am just another fool
to still believe in the power

of lost love.

BALANCE

Love is a balance
between losing and winning.

Between getting the wind
knocked out of you
and catching your breath
when something memorable happens.

So don't tell me
you expected us
to be perfect.

Don't tell me
you didn't see this coming.

(The liquor pours as I write.)

Sometimes
you're going to be
the one causing the hurting,

while other times
you're going to find yourself
awake in the middle of the night
in pain.

That's life.
That's love.

You cannot possibly believe
you were going
to come out of it the same.

Love has a tendency
to change people's lives.

People's perspectives
by putting them
in both positions
at the same time.

You're going to break people
and people are going
to break you

but in the end,
it's all for something,

to reveal
that the great secret
of it all
is to love yourself.

To put your happiness
before others.

After all,
the goal is to find someone
who knows who they are.
Someone who appreciates

their solitude

and

someone who loves themselves
just as much
as you.

WAKING UP RAW

Sometimes
you wake up,

and you just know
it's going to be
a shit day.

While other times
you inhale
and feel

the flow of the universe
passing
through your lungs.

ROBERT M. DRAKE

TO YOU, MY FRIEND

Not all men
are out to get you.

Some of them
genuinely want
to get to know you.

Some of them
actually care.

So you had a few
bad experiences,
but that doesn't mean
all men are assholes.

Some of them
do want a woman
to hold on to.

To talk to about their feelings.
To be themselves, you know?

What?
You thought women
were the only ones who cried?
Who went through shit?
Who broke down
and felt

as if they were alone?

This is the bullshit
the media wants us to believe—
that we are so different.

That none of us are equal.
Not emotionally or spiritually,

but they are *DEAD WRONG.*

Both men and women
are the same.

Both men and women
need hands
to mend them
when they feel broken.

Lips to heal their wounds.
Both men and women
need love, real love
no matter who fucks whom over,
you know?

So whether it's now
or later,
someone who cares
or someone who doesn't.

You still have to keep going,

and as you do,
remember
to pay attention
to the way people treat other people,

and make sure
you keep the ones
who are willing protect your heart
no matter what.

People need other people
to survive...

without each other,
human life is wasted.

Without each other,
human life is meaningless.

Together we have to protect
what we have

and together
we have to protect our future

no matter what.

HARD FAILURE

There are some things
that must happen
because they must.

Things you can't avoid.

Like growing up,
failure, grief,
happiness, etc.

But when it comes down
to it,
life is really about people.

It's about who you meet
and who you don't.

Who forgets you
and who remembers.

Who you run after
and who chases you down the line.

It's about who's there
when you feel most alone
and who's not.

Who you could talk to

and who makes it hard
for you to be yourself.

That's what's important.

People.

The way they look
into your eyes
right before they're gone
and the way they smile
right back at you
when you return
back home.

People,
it's always about
people.

Theones,
who love you,
protect you
and the ones who are there
for you

when you need them most.

I hope you
never forget that.

I hope you pass

this tiny bit of information
to your children.

Imagine that,

a world full of
compassion:

What a beautiful thing
it can be
for the human race.

OPINIONS & PROBLEMS

Of course,
anyone would tell you
to move on.

Anyone would tell you
it's not worth the time
and effort to make it work.

But not everyone
has gone through
what you've gone through,

despite

what you've told them.

Sometimes
people can't walk
in other people's shoes,
but for some reason

everyone's got
a mother fucking opinion.

Everyone's got
a solution to *your* problems
but no one really understands
how you feel,

how other people feel,
and how they feel
themselves.

People don't get it
although,
sometimes they want to
but they don't.

You've got your own problems,
dilemmas
and not enough time
to solve them.

Which is why
you reach out
for help.

And I get it,
you know no one can actually
help you
resolve your problems

but still,

you just want someone
there to listen to you
in your time of need.

Someone to hear you out
as you collect your broken pieces.

So I'm not going to tell you
what to do.

I'm not going to tell you
to move on—to leave certain people
behind.

I'm going to sit next to you.
I'm going to cry with you.

I'm going to hold you,
and I'm going let you know
that you're not alone.

I'm your friend
and I'll always be here
to lift you off the ground
when you need it most,

when life begins
to weigh you down,
you feel me?

I love you
and I'll never let you go.

And I'll never let
your world burn

without trying
to put out its flames.

DO WHAT YOU MUST

You've got to understand

that sometimes

words aren't enough.

That actions
should represent you

and

that people
will always judge you
based on both.

So you've got to do you,
no matter what.

You've got to
raise your middle finger

and shine

regardless of how
you make
people feel.

MORE ADVICE

You've got to
do what's right
for you
because in the end,
life goes on.

People lose interest
and you deserve
to live your life
to the fullest

every day.

THIS WAY ONLY

And I am sorry
about a lot of things
these days,

but I am not sorry

for who I am,
for the choices
I've made,

and for the way
I've learned
to let go.

I am me
and my skin
is my skin.

And accepting that
has brought me
closer to who I am
than who I ever was
to begin with.

CONVICTIONS

I know you're someone
with convictions
and so am I,
everyone gets their hands
dirty one way
or another.

Everyone has done something
they regret.

So who am I
to judge you
for what you've done.

Who am I to say
you're wrong
when I've probably done
the same things.

I'm not any better than you.
I'm not better than anyone.

I'm human
and in this aching body
I carry so many heavy things.

I carry love,
pain, fear, confusion.

And I don't know what I want.
I don't even know who I am.

I have mysteries in me
that need to be solved—
things that need to come out,
and like you,
I'm not looking for someone
who's perfect.

I'm not looking for a lover either
or for a fling that's over
by sunrise.

No.

I'm looking for acceptance.
For loyalty.
For friendship
beyond what's manufactured around us.

I'm looking for something real,
someone who's been through hell
and back.

Someone who knows
what it's like to be defeated.

I'm asking for too much,
I know,
because to be honest,

I'm not sure want I want.

I just hope whoever comes my way
is someone I deserve.

Someone who comes back
no matter how far
away they go.

WHAT YOU ARE NOT

You're not weak
and with a heart like that—
you deserve the world.

You deserve rare people:

The ones who look into your eyes
and discover your soul—the ones
who see who you really are.

But for reasons unknown,
it's always the kindest people
who get fucked over
the hardest.

It's always those
who look out for others
who get ignored
and taken for granted
the most.

And that's how you feel.

Like you're living your life
the wrong way
because you care too much,
you feel too much,
but it's not you.

My god,
it's never been you.

It's just,
most people don't see
eye to eye with you.

Most people
haven't been through enough,
so they don't understand.

Most people
only appreciate you
before they have you
and the moment right after
you're gone.

It stings, I know,
but that's what we were born into:

A life where the heart
never gets what it wants.

A life that's designed
to beat you down
no matter how much love
you spread.

And yes,
the times are relentless
but you have to keep it real

with yourself,
and if loving too much
is what you are,
then by all means necessary,
fuck everyone

and keep doing you.

You have to believe
in the love inside of you
even if no one is there
to witness it

as it blooms.

IT IS HARD

I know it's hard
letting the people
you grew up with go.

Watching them slowly fade
into their own lives
and not being able
to have a say.

I know it's hard
watching the love of your life
pass you by
without making eye contact—
without sharing
a single word.

I know it's hard
going through life
accepting these two things
while knowing
you could have done
a little more.

It's hard, all of it is.

Letting go
to let back in
to watch it leave

all over again.

It's hard,
it's always hard
and what's even harder is,
knowing how real it was
and letting it slip away
because you had to

because there was no other choice.

That's love.

Setting them free
because you care about
their happiness more
than you do
your very own.

Because deep down inside,
you know that if it's meant to be
then eventually
they'll find their way back.
And if they don't

then they were never yours
to claim
as your own.

Knowing this truth
changes everything

and there is
nothing more difficult
to accept

other

than that.

Friends leave.
They disappear
and sometimes
the bravest thing
in the world is

accepting their friendship
as you realize the moment

they are gone.

BREAKS MY HEART

It breaks my heart
to know
that one day
you will no longer be
a child.

That one day,
you will be
all grown up with a life
of your own.

That one day,
you'll go through pain
and have to figure things out
all by yourself.

It hurts
and no matter what you do,
something will always hurt.

Like when you realize
how people
are not what they seem.

That sometimes friends
are not really your friends
and that sometimes
a lover

doesn't know a thing
about love.

My dear,
it breaks my heart to know
that one day,
I'll be too old,
too weak to hold you
when you feel most alone.

That one day,
I won't be here
and that one day,
you'll have to accept
the harsh realities of grief,
of disappointment
and of moving on.

It sounds terrible doesn't it?

All these things you don't understand.

All these things
no human should ever
look forward to.

But my dear,
I want you to know
that brokenness,

isolation,

heart break
and tears

are not all that horrible.

That sometimes
you find yourself
in the mayhem of love—

in the mayhem of chaos
and nothingness.

That sometimes
losing yourself
and losing someone
may lead to a new wonder,
one filled with endless possibility.

In short,
the future is always undetermined,
and love is delicate enough
to slip through your hands.

And sometimes
the greatest people are reborn
of the deepest fires

that flare from the pain
only a human heart

can endure.

I DO NOT WANT

I don't know
what it is I want,
but I can tell you
what I don't want.

I don't want people
who take other people
for granted.

I don't want people
who pretend to care
but when it's time to show face
their true colors emerge.

I don't want to live in a world
filled with terror,
a place where I don't feel safe,

where I don't
feel at home.

I don't want small talk,
meaningless conversation,
and I don't want to lose

love

the moment I find it.

I don't want my heart
to stop chasing a dream.

I don't want to agree
with everything that's in front of me

and I don't want
any part in fake love.

I don't want what's easy,
a world covered with lies
to make me feel better
about myself.

I don't want the bullshit,
and I don't,
because I know
I deserve more.

I know I deserve
to overcome all things
that destroy life,

all things that make
all pain forgettable.

I may not know
what it is I want…

but I do know
what I don't want,

and I hope I never
let you slip away.

I hope our hands find each other
no matter where we go.

That is the science of living.

To not know
but to know what it is
you *need*
instead of what you want.

SORRY TWICE

I'm sorry you've had to deal
with your past,
with the people
you have given yourself to
and the ones
who have carelessly left you
to drown.

I'm sorry about your pain,
about what keeps you awake
at night,
about what keeps your mind
restless.

I'm sorry about your petals,
for the way they have fallen,
and for the way
the wind has blown them
away.

I know those are
your broken pieces,
and it haunts me
watching you
having to fix yourself—
to heal alone.

That sort of thing

breaks my heart.

It makes me feel
some kind of way,
it makes me feel
connected to you.

I look at you—your eyes,
your soul,
and I can't help but to think
why is it
that these types of things
always happen
to good people...

and because of that,
I feel you.

I feel you with all feeling,
all heart,
and all the moons within my soul.

And it hurts me,
it hurts all of me
to see you go through this
while believing you are
unloved.

And that's sad, you know?

It's sad

because you stand by that—
the feeling of being
unloved,
alone and forgotten.

You're not.

It's just
the wrong people
will always make you feel
this way
and the right ones
will hold your hand,

point you
toward the light
and guide you back home.

Your past shouldn't ruin
your future,
it should give you the lessons
needed

to cure everything
that hurts.

YOU FOUND

That's how it was.

Sometimes
you found yourself falling
in love with the things
you knew
you couldn't have—
with the people
who weren't good for you.

And it didn't matter at what age.

Whether you were mature
or immature.

Old or young.

Wise as an owl
or dumb as bricks.

People from all places
always found themselves
under this problem,
and at least
once in their lifetime, too.

It was always
what broke you

that attracted you
the most—what you couldn't have,
what you weren't
allowed to touch, you know?

That's what made
most people fall in love.

The fact
that they were so close
to it
but pushed back
the moment they believed
it was theirs.

Love always gave us
a reality check.

It confirmed
how hard it was to find

and how hard it was

to maintain.

COLLECTION

I am
what I am.

A collection
of both the things
I love
and the things
I do not know.

Of both
the freedom I deserve
and the confusion
that burdens me.

I am
what I am.

A deep blend of rebellion
and order
and of the craving
to be held.

I am
what I am.

The fear of being let go
and the wrath that comes
behind it.

I am hard, yet soft.
I am tough, yet gentle.

I am unfuckwithable
and gullible enough to
be taken advantage of.

I am
what I am.

I am…
a home filled with
broken windows.

I am…
a lost soul looking for
its body.

I am every man,
every woman and child.

I am no gender.
No sex.
No heritage
or race.

I am
what I am…

I am you
and you are me.

People among people.
People, oceans of them,
lost, searching for breath.

Searching for other people
who feel like them.

I am
what I am.

and I am

not here.

STILL STANDING

I am still standing
no matter
how many times
I've fallen.

No matter
how many wounds
I've obtained.

And

no matter
how many times
I've been told
I couldn't let go,

and yet,
I have.

I am standing,
still.

Alone, at last…

and I am stronger than
I was…

smarter, quieter.

The grace of God
surrounds me

and the flames of hell
chase me...

but here I am,
standing still...

and fighting against all odds

as I've always

done.

PEOPLE END

I don't know anything
about people,
about relationships.

I don't know
how things start
or how they end,
why they end.

I don't know
the chemistry that happens
between lovers,
and what keeps them
wanting more
and more and more...

no matter how bitter
things get.

All I know is
that it happens.

That people form these strange
little connections
with other people
and that makes things better.

That sometimes,

one person
can bring out the best in you
and that sometimes,
that same person
can trigger the worst of you.

It happens.

People bring out
different sides of you
and no one really knows why.

No one really understands it
and still,

people fall in love
as the sadness
never quite detaches itself
from their eyes.

It just keeps on going
until there is nothing left
to break,

nothing left to hurt.

People form these strange
little connections
with other people,

and my god,

does it almost kill them
but never
do they ask why.

AFFECT YOU

Sometimes
you can't explain
what you see in people,
what makes you
fall into them.

That's something
that happens on its own.

But you can control
the outcome.

You can control
how things go,
how they affect you,
hold you.

You have the ability
to choose your *own happiness,*
to move on
if the situation isn't right.

People tend to forget that.

They forget
that happiness
is a choice
and sometimes

the right person finds them
when they're not

looking at all.

ASK YOURSELF

You've got to ask yourself
what you're living for,
who you're living for,
and if none of those answers
begin with you,

then you're living your life
wrong.

You're living a lie.

Everything you do
should revolve around you.

Every person,
every place,
every moment

should start
and end with you.

This is your life
and you shouldn't spend it
on dull things,
on people who don't
understand the type of love
you carry
within your bones.

Because you only live once
and it's your job
to make it count.

Let every day
be yours.

So own it
and *never apologize*
for being
who you are.

ROBERT M. DRAKE

LOOK AT YOU

I look at you,
you look at me,

and something happens.

I feel
like myself
more than I ever have.

I feel
like I belong
and for the first time,

I am free.

BRING THE WALL

You don't have to
put your guard up
all the time.

Sometimes
it's okay to be vulnerable.

It's okay to break a little,
to spring from the depths
of your own wounds.

To bloom,
to grow
from all the things that hurt—
from all
the people who've caused you harm.

It only means
that you care,
that you love
and you do so,
so delicately.

I admire that about you.

The way you hold
your heart
with tender hands

and still
find it in you to protect it,
to defend it
no matter what happens.

You're strong, baby,
but with me,
you don't have to put up a fight.
There's no war here.

No battle within me…
just old defeats,
soft tragedies,
and a sad story of a hero
rising from the ashes
to save the one he loves.

The typewriter bangs
over slow melodies
filled with melancholia.

In other words, baby,
I've seen it all.

I've felt it all
and I'm exhausted.

I just want to rest in your arms
and love you

the best way I know how.

TIME AND TRUTH

When I am with you,
I forget everything.

I forget who I am,
where I'm going.

I forget what I'm supposed
to be doing and thinking.

If I'm supposed
to be here or there.

I'm not sure.

I don't know.
I can't recall it
and I can't seem
to make sense of anything
other than the way
I feel about you, kid.

You see,
I think about you
all of the time
and I can't seem
to remember any truth

other than that.

SHORE LINES

Some people
have a special
connection with the ocean.

They see themselves
in the water
and find the dreams
they've lost

on the shore.

NO CONTROL

This is your life.

You choose
who to let in,
who to let out.

You choose
who gets to love you,
who gets to destroy you,
break you
beyond repair.

You choose
who to walk out on
or who to stay with
'til the very end.

This is your world,
your interpretation of it,
and these are your feelings

that *only you* can recognize.

And these are your scars
left behind
by the people you love,
the people you choose
to hurt you.

You control the direction
you go through.

You know
what's right
and what's wrong
because like I said,

this is your life
and no one knows it better
than you...

and you deserve
what's best for you

or

nothing at all.

WHAT I WISH

Sometimes,
I wish you could put yourself
in my shoes.

I wish
you could have seen it
from my perspective,

to feel what I felt,
to be a stranger
in your own heart.

If so,
then perhaps,
it wouldn't have been
that hard on me,
that easy on you.

Perhaps,
we could have found
a mutual ground,
some place strong enough
for the both of us
to stand on.

But no,
you had to be you
and I had to be me

and we had to fuck each other
up a little harder,
a little rougher
than our past relationships.

I wanted to save you
and you wanted to save me,
but of course,
that's not how it went down.

That's not how it happened
despite
the good intensions
we had from the start.

That shit *never* goes
the way you envisioned it.

Hell,
it doesn't even get close…
and now,
I know that,

and I wish I could have
done things differently from the start.

Perhaps,
we could have been better
and all the promises
we made
could have come true.

We could have been
two people

who weren't
like everyone else.

Imagine that.

Imagine if we
had stayed together...

I would not have
been writing this

poem.

FACTS

Sadly,
no matter how many people
you meet,

it's the ones
who let you down
who get the best parts
of you.

TIME STARTS

People don't come across
each other by accident.

It has been written
in the stars.

Therefore,
theoretically,

I have been waiting for you
since the beginning of time.

Since God lifted
his index finger
and extracted the expanding universe.

I will always belong to you
even after

it all stops.

SOMETIMES YOU DO

You have to
walk away sometimes.

You have to know
when it's time to move on,
to let go

because that's the hardest part.

Realizing how people change,
how you change
and how sometimes
even staying is wrong—
even when your heart
is telling you

it's the right thing
to do.

ACCEPTANCE

You don't need acceptance,
permission to be yourself.

You don't need to apologize
or be careful with the way
you think or feel.

You don't need
the comfort of people
who don't appreciate
what you carry within
that beautiful heart of yours.

You don't need fake love
or fake friends,

and by that,
I mean,
people who think
they know
what it's like to burn.

The ones who have no idea
what it's like
to break softly
in the middle of the night,
to weep silently,
to hold everything within

as the world slowly passes
them by.

That's not the kind of people
you need.

You need people
who stay silent by you
when you don't have the words
to describe how you feel.

People who invite themselves
when you feel alone,

who notice,
who take action
when you think there's not enough
to do.

That's who you need,
my love,

people who are willing
to hold you up
whenever you feel
as if you're

about to fall.

ALL PLACES

I am always
looking for you
in all places that remind me
of our past

and although

I know you're not coming,
I find myself,
with all that I am,

in search of you again.

Between what was
and what never will be.

I am
always falling more
in love

with all the ghosts

you have left
behind.

FAULT

It's not your fault,
it never has been.

The thing is,
sometimes the heart
deceives you.

Sometimes
it leads you toward
the wrong situation,
toward the wrong kind
of love.

And it does so
to teach you,
to bless you with lessons
of sacrifice,
forgiveness
and those of patience.

So you should never
take these things for granted
because these types of things
must happen regardless
if you're a good person or not.

People fall in and out of love
and sometimes,

in the long run,
the most painful parts
of watching someone go
can be the most life changing.

It can lead you
toward that person
who's meant to take the hurt away.

So whether it hurts now or later,
you must always believe

that someone better
is on the way.

I WONDER

I'm jealous
and I am because
you give yourself
to people
who don't know your worth,

to people
who don't appreciate you
or your time.

And it makes me wonder,
you know?

Why?

Why in the world
would such a beautiful person
put themselves
through so much pain?

I don't get it.

You have everything in front of you.

Everyone you need,
people who adore you
and love you.
People you've over looked.

Open your eyes,
sweet one.
The people you spend
most of your time thinking of,
stressing over,
don't want you.

Hell,
they barely even notice
when you're not around

and still,

you want to believe that it's
the kind of love you deserve,

the kind of attention
you should chase
because it's all you've ever known...

but it's wrong,
all of it is.

You don't deserve to believe
that you need
to have people that shatter you
to feel alive.

You don't deserve
that kind of broken love.
You deserve sad songs

with happy endings.

You deserve the deepest love,
someone who'll look at you
and echo your name forever.

Someone
who'll be there for you
and risk everything they have
for the chance
to wake up next to you...

to look you in the eyes...

and know
that they belong
to you

and vice versa.

TELL ME

Tell me how many people
have hurt you.

Tell me about the scars
you carry,
the ones you've had
a hard time forgetting about,

the ones that keep reminding you
of how fragile you really are.

Tell me about what breaks you,
who has broken you
and why sometimes
you find yourself dwelling in pain.

Tell me about your past.

Who you've given your heart to
and who has broken it,

who has cared for it
and who has left it behind
without regret.

Tell me about the spark of hope
in your eyes
and tell me what you're hiding

behind that gentle smile.

Tell me why
you're the way you are
and what makes you feel
the things you feel.

Tell me about what you need,
what you think
you want
and what's enough for you
to get by.

Tell me about love:

if you've felt it,
lost it
or if you've been close to it,
enough to recognize it
from afar.

Tell me how you feel
about me.

If I cross your mind
in the middle of the night
and if I accompany you
when you feel most alone.

Tell me all these things
about you

before the moon comes crashing down,
before breath
escapes my lungs
and before I lose my sanity
to the world.

Tell me,
and I will tell you

why you are the most
important person in your life,
and how you should never doubt
yourself,
no matter what you say
or do.

You have to trust yourself
more than anyone else.

You have to ask yourself
these questions
and know

that you are the only
person capable

of answering them

as well…

YOUR LIFE

Your life
isn't meant to be perfect.

It isn't meant
to be all happiness
or all sadness.

Your life
is about finding yourself
in the middle,
inbetween what gives you
life
and what destroys you.

It's about
finding balance,
about
evenly distributing
both bad and good things,

both bad and good people.

And it's not meant
to be easy, no never that...

but it is also not meant
to be very hard.
Though

most of the time
it does feel that way,
but it's not.

And I know
almost everyone you know
will tell you
how you have to find
what's good for you,
what's best for you,
what makes you happy, etc.

And it is usually
when you feel the complete opposite.

When you feel
like death is right around
the corner.

But the truth is,

you have to live your life.
You have to figure things out
on your own

even if they're bad for you.

You have to,

and you have to alone
because the key is

to keep going.

To keep improving yourself
no matter how much you fail
or prevail.

LikeI said,
your life isn't meant to be perfect.

It's meant
to be fulfilling
and in the end,
you learn from all the mistakes
you made.

You strive
and you never question the things
that happened.

You never question
the people who ruined you
or made you better.

You just look back
and thank yourself

for pulling through.

I NEED YOU

I need you to understand
that before I give myself
to you…

I must first discover
who I am.

I need you to understand
that before I give my heart
to you…

I must first
break it myself
to know how it works,
how it heals.

I need you to understand
that before I love you…

I must first
love myself,
to know how it feels,
what it's like to be complete.

I need you to understand
that before I give you
all of my hours…
I must first

find complete solitude
in me,
absolute peace
and comfort in my own skin.

I need you to understand
that before anything happens…

I must first
understand that I allowed it
to happen,
that there are no coincidences,
that I am in full control
of my life
and no one else's.

So before you attempt
to knock on my door,

understand

that I am me,
that I am liberated
and I need someone who understands.

Someone who is at peace
with themselves
before trying to settle in.

I need someone
who's willing to walk with me

and not follow
my footsteps as I lead.

Amen.

HUMAN ROOMS

It is
a beautiful thing
for the human heart
to let people go
because it is
only making room
for others.

So do not feel
too badly,
it is only natural
to outgrow things,
to outgrow people,
places,
and art.

It is only natural
to feel disconnected
from things
you were once connected to.

Doing so
proves that you are alive,
that you are moving forward
the way you were supposed to.

So dear,
do not be so hard

on yourself,

let go and forget.

Let go and let in.
Let go and forgive.
Let go and grow.

It only means
you have so much more
to look forward to.

So much more
than you are used to

and so much more
than you'll ever know.

Let go
and do it gracefully.

and know
that out of this…

beautiful things
may come.

BREAKING PAPER

I don't relate to people
who break other people,
to people
who use others
for their own gain,
for their own amusement.

I'm sorry.
I'm a different kind of person.

I care,
I try
and I don't give up
on the people I love.

And although
sometimes,
I am hard on them,

I am constantly reminded
of how blessed I am
because of them.

So yeah,
take your shit and go.

I don't need that kind
of negativity,

that kind of love
that destroys precious things.

I have my people
right here
and every day we are drinking,
laughing
and celebrating life itself
the proper way.

So please, be gone.

Please vanish
before my tired eyes
because I'm right
where I should be,

with whom
I'm supposed to be

and I don't need you.

I never have.

I ADMIRE YOU

Some people
get the best of you,
and it's okay
because it's not your fault
if it doesn't work out.

But still,
I admire you for what you do,
knowing how people are,
knowing that some of them
are only in it for themselves.

I respect that.

No matter how many times
you've been hurt,
you still give people chances
because you believe in change,
in the greater good.

You believe that no matter
how bad it gets,
that if you work with them,

eventually
you'll see results.
That's hope.

You don't give up on people.
You fight with them,
even if they've lost

hope

themselves.

You deserve
a goddamn medal for this.

For overseeing the bullshit,
for convincing people of how
beautiful they are.

I admire you.

Never change for anyone.

DO NOT BE SORRY

Don't be sorry
for what you've done.

All of us
have some hard decisions
to make.

All of us
have lost someone
who meant the world
to us

at the cost
of our own happiness.

This is how it works.

Sometimes,
you have to do things
for yourself
no matter how arrogant it is.

Sometimes,
You have to put yourself first.

You have to build your own castle
before helping others
build theirs.

I KNOW THIS

Yes,
I know
it is true.

Some people
are meant to slip away
the moment
you believe they are yours

and most of the time,

you're left alone
haunted by their memories.

And they never quite
go away
at least not quietly…

They just
sort of linger

as time goes on.

I NEED SOMEONE

Sometimes
you just need someone
to talk to.

Someone
to pour yourself into.

That's the beauty
of having a best friend.

You can find them
at any given moment

and you just know
they'll always be there.

MISS ME ALWAYS

I hope you will miss me
and think of me.

And I hope you will remember me
for the way I loved you,
for the way I smiled
when I was broken down,
and for the way
I took one last look at you
before I found myself gone.

I hope you will take the time
to look back
and appreciate what we had,
and I hope your heart finds
what it deserves.

I hope you don't feel
the sorrow,
the rain that swallows you whole,

and I hope
isolation doesn't find you.

I hope you don't taste
the bitterness of loneliness
and I hope
you don't find yourself

missing the company
of another person.

This is the type
of burning that never leaves
one's soul.

And I am on fire.

My flesh,
my bones and my soul
are on fire.

Because I was too late.

Too late to realize this…

that sometimes,
the best thing you can do
to someone
is

set them free.

NOT ALL

Not all good-byes
are harsh and hard.

Some good-byes
can be meaningful
and beautiful.

Some can be life changing,
they can make you
or break you.

They can give you
the courage to heal,
to move on,

to forgive and love
yourself fiercely.

The truth is,

you learn a little more
about yourself
every time someone says

good-bye.

RIGHT NOW

Right now
you feel alone
but you should know
that there are still

a lot of good people
out there worth loving.

You just have to
go through several bad ones

to find the ones
worth drowning for.

I AM I AM

I am speaking to you,
writing to you,

to let you know
that you're not alone.

To let you know
that I, too,
feel empty at times,
no matter how many blessings
I've received.

No matter how good it's been.

I don't know what it is
that is meant to fill
this void,
this starved heart.

At times,
I feel like I am spiraling down
this dark well
to only greet the ocean below…

one
I know
I'm not suited for.

I don't have
the strength to swim.

I am exhausted
from trying to figure things out,

from trying to live up to what others
want me to be.

So you're not alone.
You never were.

Not physically,
emotionally or spiritually.

You have people here
with you who care.

People who are willing
to give you
your space when you're trying
to figure out the stars
in your head…

and that's a blessing

whether you know it
or not.

You're never quite alone
no matter how far you go,

and you should never regret
opening up to people
who know
what it's like
to be in your shoes.

NEVER SAY IT

You should never
expect to find
a piece of yourself

in the same place
you felt lost.

The same way
you should never

expect to find love
in the same people

who left you
broken.

POWER IS...

You're not
what they want you to be.

You're not
the labels people put on you,
and you're not
what you fear,
what they fear.

You're not
your past,
although,
you should never forget it.

And you're not
your flaws:

the errors they catch
and the scars that break you
every once in a while.

You're not any of that.
You're so much more,
regardless
of your faults...

because you've got something
most people don't have

and *that's guts,* kid.

You inhale,
take it all in
and never think twice
of their opinions.

That's power.

Your world is made of confidence
and fire,

and the only one
who could destroy it

is you.

BEYOND THIS

You've got to
take everything they say,
good or bad
and carry it
behind your back
like a pair of wings.

You've got to fly,
my love,
find adventure
beyond this city.

You've got to move on,
find yourself
in places you never knew existed.

You've got to meet
new people,
the ones who know
more about you
than yourself.

The ones you never thought
you'd meet.

You've got to find
your perfect freedom,
my love,

expand your arms,
and dominate your life
with no fear.

You've got to believe
that there's still a fight in you.

So take it, my love.
Know it, my love.

Understand that your life
is the most precious thing
in the world
and know

that there is nothing
more beautiful

than experiencing
the love of another person.

DEATH COMES

I must have died
last year
because I can no longer feel.

Now this is when
things get real.

When you feel
like you've been dead all year long,
not being able
to feel.

Not being able
to know what it is
that you're missing.

This is how it sparks.

Like one day,
you're living your life
and loving your life

and then
it hits you
like a ray of light.

It hits you
but not hard enough

to notice the impact.

That is when things change.

When people
begin to move their mouths
but you don't hear the words
being projected.

This is what it's like
to be left alone.

To be loved one day
to only be a burden
the next.

That is what it's like
to walk a thousand miles
and not find your way
back home.

To tell someone
you love them
and not hear it
in return.

The world ends
and all that is left
are the burning memories.

The ones you've aired out

and the ones
you've drowned
in the river of your veins.

This is the void.

The lost space scientist cannot explore.

The new low.
The deepest parts
of your heart.

This is how it ends.

The moment you realize
the person you love
no longer feels the same way.

Your legs are still.
Your arms are still.
Your eyes and face,
still,

and all that is left
is what you carry inside
and it sinks within you
like a weight
piercing through the sheets,
the layers of your soul.

I can no longer feel,

adapt.

I can no longer hurt,
cry.

I've gone beyond those things,
beyond what this
human experience guarantees.

I must have died last month
and now,
I am waiting where the gods await,

where perfection
and sorrow collided.

Where stars go to die
where only the lonely reside.

I am a fool.
Yes,
that I am,
but I am a fool

who has once held love with care,
and now,
like the fool
that I am

I have lost it and I regret
letting it slip away.

SENSES

I have this deep sense
of feeling

that some of me
isn't real,

that some of me
isn't here

and that some of me
isn't meant

to be mended again.

THE LESS YOU...

I sometimes wonder
where all that love you had
for me went.

Did it walk out of your life?

Did you throw it away?

Or did you lose it
one night while you were alone?

And then,
after all this time,
it comes to me.

The less you gave,
the more I found.

The further you went,
the closer I was.

The less you cared,
the more I loved
and because of that
you helped me find myself.

It was one of those things
I didn't know

until now.

So thank you
for everything you never gave me.

For all the love,
attention and time
you didn't have.

I'm stronger now
and I wouldn't be who I am
without that.

This is my metamorphosis
and the change

is out of this world.

MY PAST

I can't change
my past
and I can't understand
my failures.

But I have loved you
with my mind,
body and soul,

and that
has brought me closer
to happiness

than I have ever been.

TEARS, MAN

When the tears are gone
and the gentle ache
the heart brings fades.

You will know
that it was all for something.

Therefore,
you must take this with you.

Place it in a safe place
but do not forget it is there.

Follow your path,
accept your flaws
and hold on to your heart
when things change.

You're welcome,
and watch your step.

UNDO THINGS

You can't undo things,
and you can't
go back to how things were.

What you said
has been done
and what you've done
will never come back
to you
even if you tried.

All you can do
is make peace with what you've lost.
With what you've learned
to accept of yourself.

No matter what has happened,
you're a better person...

no matter how many worlds
you've destroyed.

You're a better person...

no matter how many times
you've had to
put up with yourself
for the mistakes you've made.

The idea of tomorrow
can be a beautiful thing,

if onlyyou let
all that brings you harm

pass you by.

SO MUCH OUT OF ME

You take so much
out of me
but also put
so much back in me.

And that is why
I love you.

I exhale,
you inhale,
and never do I experience
the same breath twice.

You give me life
in all, unforgiving places.

In the water, I am yours.

In the air, I am yours.

In the flames,
and in the places
I have yet to discover.

And never
have I been able
to envision

what my life would be like

without the thought
of you.

THE GROUND FALLS

The ground is solid
and the air is thin.

I fall. I fall. I fall.

And this is what
growing up
must feel like.

Like seeing,
and knowing,

how everything
fucked up can possibly happen
to you beforehand

and still
charge straight toward it
with a smile.

Responsibility is a bitch
and life
is just another metaphor

for pain.

MOST PEOPLE

Most people are exhausted.

They're tired of the horrors
life brings.

Which is why
most
don't want to read
about darkness.

There's too much pain
going around lately,
too much
human suffering.

People want to heal.

They want peace.

They want to be left alone.

They crave something positive,
anything,
to help them
get through their day.

People need light
just as much as they need

darkness.

They need something to
distract them

from the pain they carry
within.

DO NOT

Do not fall in love with me.

I am not easy
to love
and I know
it might be a bad thing

because I know
I demand so much.

I'm not the softest person
and I have
a whole goddamn list
of things
I require.
And none of them
come easy.

Most of them are hard.
Most of them
aren't for the faint hearted.

I have standards
because I know
what I want, what I deserve
and I know
what I have to offer.
I'm a cloudy day,

the soft rain above the sea,
the last breath
from a warm good-bye.

I'm all sadness combined
in one person,

all tears
that fall from tired eyes
and all things
that wrap around a broken heart.

What I am trying to say is

I'm not perfect
and I don't expect you
to be either,

but I know my worth.

And I love
with all tenderness,
carefulness
and with everything I do not know
about myself.

I just want something real.

Someone
who isn't afraid
of what goes on within,

and I demand nothing less
than that.

I know who I am
and I know
how everything ends
and begins with me.

So please,
do not fall in love with me…

I know
you can do so much better
than that.

YOUR HEART

That's who your heart
belongs to.

The last person
you think of
right before
you fall asleep

and the first person
you think of
when you wake.

That's who your heart
belongs to…

take notice of this
and remind them
of how much

you need them
before

they are gone.

NO ONE UNDERSTANDS

No one understands you.

Well,
of course not.

We all feel this way
and to some degree
we don't expect
to be understood,

but we do expect
someone to be there.

Someone
with enough patience
to try,
to break us down
to the very core
of ourselves.

This is what makes
life beautiful.

To have people
try…

and try and try
to be there for you…

to try to save you
even if they know

they cannot.

AND NOW

And now,
when I look into your eyes,
I feel something,
and I don't necessarily know
what it means.

But I do know it stings.
It hurts.

It stirs the waters
from the soul.

And sometimes
it feels as if my life
is being dragged out of my body,
pulled into another realm,
another dimension.

The thing is,
you left a lot of pain in me,
darling.

In my eyes and hands,
and because of it
my fingers are broken.

I'm too fragile.
I can't find love

in another person.
I can't hold on to another heart.

I don't have it in me, baby.

And now,
since you've been gone,
almost everyone I meet
thinks
they can heal me,
thinks
they have enough in them
to fix me,

to bring me back
to what I once was.

I hate that.

I hate that I've become
a task, a puzzle
wanting to be solved,
and I can't stand it.

I'm broken man,
a mad man
lost in a sea of lost love.

Barely hanging on,

but those eyes of yours...

they make me smile.

They bring out
the innocence in me.

They bring out
these familiar feelings
I think I've felt before.

It's stupid, I know,
but no one ever told me
this is what
it would be like.

No one ever told me
that a women's eyes
are deeper than all the oceans

and how
even the strongest of men
can drown.

Those eyes
have stripped my flesh
bare to the bone,

and now
there is nothing left of me
to see.

You had me

all this time
while I was out looking for myself.

And now,
I am yours:

mind, body, soul and all.

And like a flower set on fire,

I embrace the flame
as the burning fragrance of defeat
fills the air.

I love you

and sometimes, love
comes to this.

To slow deaths
and slow burnings

and no one in the world
can ever explain

why.

IT BEGINS

And yes,
I have failed
at many things,
but this is not
how it ends.

This is how it begins.

This is how
I shatter
intoa million different pieces,
to discover myself
a million different ways.

This is my time,
my awakening,

and I can feel
the universe spinning

on the tip
of my tongue.

BEEN HERE BEFORE

We've been here before,
and we both know
very well how it goes,
how it ends.

And still,
we wonder what it is all for,
what does it all mean
and why do we continue
to do it.

Why do we continue
to put ourselves
through so much pain.

Love and life.

This hurting,
breaking
and the ache it leaves behind.

We know a little
too much of what to expect
from love
and a lot less
of who we are,

to the point

where we are
looking for who we are
in other people's lives,
ideas and expectations.

I want to love you,
I do,
but I know far too much
of how it would affect me,
of how it would bury me
beneath the earth

the moment it all goes
to shit.

And it will
because it always does.

We have this urgency
of finding love,
of giving love
and not knowing
a goddamn thing about love
to begin with.

And then we ask ourselves
why we are crazy,
why we are numb
and empty

because

we've been here before
and yet,

it all feels different every time.

Love and life.
Life and love.

It is all the same.

Chaos and laughter.
Laughter and death.

It is all the same.

People and places.
Places and memory.

It is all the same.

That person in the mirror
and who you dream of being
one day.

It is all the same,

but in all aspects
it makes you real.

So yes,
we've been here before,

you and I.

We know how this is going to end,
and
the beauty of it is,

although
it is not meant to last forever,
we fight hard
for that one moment

that is meant
to take our breaths away.

One love, my sweet people.

Find it,
even if you lose
everything you love.

ALONE IN THE NIGHT

If being alone
has taught me anything,
it has taught me

how to be strong
when needed,

how to let go
when there's nothing left
to hold on to,

and how to value myself

before giving my love
to anyone else.

HERE I STAND

Here I stand,
thinking, wondering,
if anyone
feels what I feel.

If anyone grieves
and hurts the way I hurt.

And so,
it comes to me
as if I am the last person
on the planet.

As if I am the only person
looking at the flowers,
daydreaming
about the beautiful people
I've lost.

As if I am the last one left
with a handful of scars
and a long list of regrets,
buried beneath the last song
I sang.

This pain does not define me
but in all honesty,
who am I?

I ask
as all things that end
haunt my last breaths.

What is this delicate sadness
that fights gently into our hearts?

Tell me what does it all mean?

*Why does it sting
the way it stings?*

Tell me about these fingerprints,
the ones that have made a home
out of my heart.

And tell me why I can still remember
a little of my past.

Am I supposed to let go
or hold on?

Am I supposed to fall on purpose?

Knowing
I am not strong enough to fly?

I ask,
if I am really here.

If all of this darkness

is real,
if any of it
is any good for me.

No one seems to know.

No one seems to even care.

And this is how
my meaning finds its way
into my life.

This is how
and when it all makes sense.

It is in all the moments
I feel lost…
when I am mostly full of self-doubt,
questions
and insecurities

where I find myself.

Where I recognize my smile.
I am an anchor
and I belong in the bottom
of the sea.
And anyone
brave enough to dive toward the bottom
will drown with their eyes closed.
I am more

than what you see

but still,
I am wondering
if anyone feels what I feel.

If anyone has died
the ways I have died

and if anyone
has been brought back
to life

by someone
who understands.

FIGURE IT OUT

You have to
figure things out
on your own.

Life is about timing.

You have to trust
what it gives you

and

make flowers
of all things
that mean you harm.

THE TWO

You have to know
that you are full,

and not half full
or almost full

but completely
from top to bottom.

You have so much
inside of you
and it is enough space

to demand more
than a couple of meteors
and stars.

You have to believe this
and understand

that emptiness
is a state of mind.

That brokenness
doesn't last long enough

and that

the flow of time
moves quicker

than you can realize
the two.

WALK AWAY

And as you walked away,
I slowly touched the void
in your soul.

And as I did,
it filled mine.

And that's what destroyed me.

(Or so I believe.)

The way I finally saw you
for who you were
but by then,

of course,
as all things that
are good to me...

it was
too late.

TIME AND TIME

Don't be so hard on yourself
when you find yourself
dwelling on your past
and overthinking
about all the misfortune
you've had.

Because sometimes
people forget
that their past is a pathway.

And a pathway is a journey.
And a journey takes time.

And time is all you have
when you feel lost.

So please be patient
and kind.

Something better
is on the way.

IT NEVER LEAVES

The emptiness never left.

It now inhabits
a smaller space in me
and sometimes

it makes me feel
like I'm the last person alive.

Empty rooms need to be filled
and empty souls do too.

And sometimes
no matter how decorated
they are…

the two always
find it within their nature

to let
all that is within
slip away.

Time passes,
and almost
always empty spaces
remain empty
all of the time.

BLACK HOLES

You shouldn't fall
because you feel heavy.

You shouldn't break
because you feel so fragile.

And you shouldn't hold on
to the first person
who lets you slip away.

Remember your worth.

This is the year
and the next

you will discover
that you are made of love,

that you are made of black holes
and other broken things.

ROBERT M. DRAKE

MADLY, FOOLISHLY IN LOVE

I am madly, foolishly
in love with you…

lost backward in you
with no escape.

And it feels
like my heart
has been pierced by flowers
instead of knifes.

For once, I feel good.

I feel invincible.
I feel like I am walking
between the space
where lighting and thunder merge.

If there has ever been a moment
to live,
it is this one.

In times
when I am with you,
thinking of you,
crying over you
and remembering you.
All meshed into one.

This sweet pain fulfills me.

It gives me hope
in times of darkness.

In times when I have
left it all
on the table.

AloneI drain myself out.

I had a hole
in the middle of my chest
and now it is gone.

Your hand has covered it
and it has given my heart
another chance.

Thank you.

THE MESSAGE

Recreate yourself,
adjust to the times
and how they change,

and don't forget
to plant flowers

in the darkest depths
of your soul.

COLD HEART

She says I'm cold,

that I do not know
how to love.

That even when I'm trying
I still
find a way to fuck things up.

I reminisce
while we're in bed,

and I collect all
that I've been through
on a whim.

I smile at my past
as I attended my wounds
and pull another arrow
from my back.

I gently laugh.
The silence fills the room
and still,

she wonders how many times
I have been shattered.

To have the audacity
to give myself to her

with a missing
heart.

YOUR LIFE

You took your life away.

Riding through airplanes,
lost and confused while
staring out of the window.

It must be hard.
It must be dark.

Confusing, that I know.

It must be lonely up there.

You must be
missing your friends,
family, my brother.

You must be imaging
how it's likewithout you there.

Wondering
if anyone is missing you.

Wondering
if what you did
was the right thing to do.

No one knows

No one ever will.

No one ever finds
their way…

and I think
most of us
are the same wayas you
or close enough.

I can only imagine, my brother.

I can only
close my eyesto be surrounded
by the darkness.

I can only lie on my bed…
to feel
what it was like…

what you felt
when you were
lying in your coffin.

My brother,
will you forgive me?

For that last night
you called
and I did not answer
becauseit was too late.

It must have been hard.
It must have been dark.

It must have been lonely,
and now the tables
have turned.

And all my life
I have been confused
about life.

All my life
I have been living backward.

I am sorry,my brother.

I cannot forgot your face,
your smile.

I cannot forget how brave
youwere.

How strong that heart was.

If I can bring you back
I would... and
if death was a place,
then I would walk across
the world to find it,

to pull you from it

and greet you in breath.

My brother,
I can only imagine.

I can only dream
of what it islike for you
on the other side.

I hope you are okay
and I hope you are
finally free

wherever
you have gone.

MOST TIMES

I feel so much
at times,

that I barely

feel anything
at all.

A PERSON

A person
is just a person

until you feel them,
spend time
with them

and understand them.

And then,
they become more

and before you know it,

it is over

in a blink of an eye.

TWO BIRDS

Well, it's sad isn't it?

The language of love,
the translation of it.

How it begins and how it ends.

Like one day you're together,
losing yourselves
in the hours, talking till 3 a.m.,
sharing secrets the world
has yet to know.

And then,
a flash happens,
and the next moment,
you're just people.

Two ordinary people
who used to know
one another.

Two ordinary people left behind.

Life is funny, you know?

It gives
and it takes

and it has no mercy,
no remorse.

It just does what it has to do,
regardless
if your feelings get hurt
or if you win or lose.

That's life.
That's love.

You just have to trust
your timing.

Trust what's handed
to you
and what's not meant
to be yours.

From people
to moments
to things.

What is yours
will always be yours

and what isn't

will slip through your hands
like hot sand.

THE HARDEST PART

The hardest part
is coming to the realization,

that no one
is really going to save you
but yourself,

that pain
is your life's most valuable teacher

and that

you will never find happiness
until you are

completely,
absurdly

in love
with yourself.

HOW LONG

I wonder how long
you would hold on
to the wrong person

until

you realize
that the only feelings
you should be

worrying about

are that
of your own.

I WONDER

I wonder if people
feel the same as me.

If they feel exiled
from their own skin.

If they feel confused
about being who they are.

And if they go through
their lives believing

they are capable
of so much more.

FLOWERS AND SCARS

I want flowers on my back
instead of scars.

I want books
instead of guns.

And I want peace
instead of war.

I want to live.

I want life
to be my only option.

I want air
to fill my lungs
and I want the smoke
from burning buildings
to fade.

I want love
but not the love
of someone else.

I want self-love.

I want hands to touch hands
and fist

to become fist
if only
to express power,
and not violence.

I want freedom
but not the freedom to go
where you want.

I want liberation of self.

I want
to become who I want
to become
and not be prosecuted
or judged over it.

I want humanity,
connectivity
even if it is only with these words.

I want to feel
without knowing what it is
I feel.

To flourish
in something new,
something undiscovered.

Like the blooming of love,
unconditional love.

That's all I want.

Greatness and connection, forever.
Love and happiness, forever.
Life and blessings, forever.

Forever.

Until the last sun
devours the dirt

and the dust in our bones
return to the stars.

TRUTH

I just want the truth.

The truth about grief,
life, loss and love.

And I don't want it
sugar coated to protect the past.

I don't want the people
I love
to hold back
about what's really going on
in order to protect me.

To save me
from some kind of terrible feeling.

I want the truth,
goddamn it, and I want it
even if it hurts.

Even if it
leads me toward my doom.

I don't want to die
with a handful of lies,
with more questions
than answers,

and I don't want to chase
something that's not there.

I'm sorry
I'm being too demanding,
but I can't help it.

I can't control the urge to know.
To break things
down to the atom and understand them.

So please,
go ahead,
take my soul
and throw it in the fire
but don't tell me
it won't hurt.

Don't tell me
it won't scorch me,
and don't tell me

I'm what you've always
been looking for—to leave
by morning.

Give me what's real,
the nitty gritty of things

because
I'd rather live with the truth

than live the rest of my life

wondering

where it all
went wrong.

ON SADNESS

How sad
it is
to fall in love
with words
instead of actions.

To break over letters
and drown in a body
of water

that doesn't exist.

ESCAPING IT ALL

Some people
get the best of you
and it's not your fault
because some people
are assholes.

That's just how it is
but still,
I admire you for what you do,

knowing how they are,
knowing that some of them
are only in it
for themselves.

And no matter how many times
you've been hurt
you still give people chances

because you believe in change,
in the greater good.

I admire that about you.

You don't know people's true intentions
and still,

you treat everyone

as you'd like to be treated.

I respect people like that,
like you.

People who give
and give and give
until there's nothing left
to give.

You deserve a crown,
a kingdom of flowers
away from the bullshit

and a pair of wings
to fly,

whenever you feel
like escaping
from it all.

SAME PEOPLE SAME MIND

We read the same books,
watch the same movies,
and visit the same places.

And yet,

we are all so different

and on many levels
we are drowning

all the same.

AND YET...

We feel,
we cry,
we crash
and burn.

And yet,
none of us
want to let go
of the things

that weigh us
down.

YESTERDAY

Be better than
yesterday.

Be better than
who you used to be
before this very moment.

And be that person
who looks back

and says:

*"I gave you the best of me
and I am still here."*

Regardless of whom you are
or who

you're meant to be.

SELF-LOVE

Love yourself.

I cannot stress it enough.

Love yourself
if it is the only thing
you do believe in.

Love yourself,
do it, but do it
because you must,
because there is
no other way to live.

No other way
to love another person.

Love yourself.

Put yourself first,
know that you are
the most important person
in your life.

Love yourself.

Fiercely and bravely,
and I know

it is one of the most
confusing things to do,
hardest things to do
but you must
learn to do so…

if you want a fair shot
at happiness.

Love yourself.

I cannot stress it enough.

Love yourself, goddamn it.

You do not have to be perfect.
You weren't born to be.

You were born to grow
through error.

To love
through heartbreak
and to live
through loss.

This is how you'll learn.
This is how you'll know,
that the greatest tragedy
in life is
believing in all the things

that break you

and not loving yourself
enough

to believe
that you are more.

VIOLENT PEOPLE

Some people
rule through violence
and power.

They must believe
that this is the only way
to move people

but they are wrong.

Fear is no blessing.
Destruction is no light.

Love is the greatest gift,
understanding connects humanity

and *kindness is everything,*

my sweet, people.

I SWEAR, MAN

That's what hurts the most.

The fact that I gave you
almost everything I had.

My time,
heart and art.

And in the end,
I got nothing,
not even a decent good-bye,

just a mouthful
of empty words
that felt
like they were missing something,
words that didn't mean
anything.

But it's all good.

I probably deserved it.
I probably caused it
on my own.

And I probably
wouldn't even be where I am
if it wasn't for you.

So I'm not sure
if I should thank you
or tell you to fuck off.

I'm not sure
if I'm in a good place
or in an even worse place
than before.

I'm not sure
if I should be happy
for having a little bit left,
perhaps even enough
to breathe

or sad
for being alone,
confused...
where the darkness dwells.

These things,
I swear, these people.

The more I give,
the more I lose.
And the more I lose
the less I feel,
the more I lose track
of myself.

And like I said,

that's what hurts
the most.

When I'm with someone I
give them 100% of myself
and it's just sad,

that still,
after all the bullshit people go through,
some people
just don't get it.

Some people take
and take and take
without ever giving back

a piece of themselves.

I swear, man…

some people make me sick.
They want everything
for themselves

but fail to give
in return.

EXPLAIN YOURSELF

You don't have to
explain yourself.

You feel
what you feel
because it's how
you're meant to feel.

Therefore,
you shouldn't ignore
that voice inside of you.

The one that knows you
more than you know yourself.

The one that manifests itself
when no one is around.

You have to trust it,
ascend with it,

and weave through the darkness
no matter what it reveals.

You have to go
where your heart leads,

trust it

and follow it
no matter how disconnected
you feel.

IMAGINE THIS

Imagine how different
your life would be.

If you had done
what you wanted to do,

or said
what you wanted to say

or kissed
all the people
you wanted to kiss
without a worry tugging
at your mind.

Perhaps,
you would be
a completely different person,

and perhaps,

you would look into the mirror
and be proud of yourself

for freeing everything
you've ever

held inside.

MISFORTUNE IT IS

What a terrible misfortune
it is,
to give what you own

and never watch it return
back home,

no matter how many signs
you leave behind.

To love
but feel unloved,

no matter how many people
you've touched.

And to believe
there's nothing out there

when in reality
there's someone waiting for you

to discover them
in every corner…

And in every moment
you didn't
give a chance to.

DARK DWELLS

This is my disconnect.

What I feel
when I don't want to feel.

When the inspiration
has slipped through my hands.

I write what my dead brother
has let go of.

What his worn hands
could no longer carry.

I'm below the earth.
Below what hurts.
Below any kind of tension
that elevates the pain.

You think the ocean is deep?

We'll come
and talk to me.

Take a glance at what it's like
to die every night.

To rise every morning

and know
what awaits when the darkness dwells.

This is what it feels like
to have the boiling sun
in the palm of your hand

and tell everyone
you know it's okay.

This is what people need to read,
to know about human nature.

The destruction,
the war, and mindless rattles
that shake their beating hearts

and the maps that lead
to nowhere.

This that circle,
the one most follow
through their lives
and call it

life.

Their feet burn.
Their lungs and heart,
too.
This is what oblivion

tastes like.

To have your tongue
lick the stars
without knowing where to rest
your head.

Without knowing
where it begins or ends.

This is the truth.

The reality people run from,
the words no one wants to accept.

The passage
through a river
filled with a thousand gators.

That is
what your mind goes through
when you're alone

and this is what hurts.

The solitude
no man should go through
on their own.

The abandonment of government
and the people who claim

you as their own.

I put this on my aunt's
dry bones and my grandmother's
dying wish.

If hell exists,
then it manifests
every time someone lets you go.

Every time someone leaves
without saying good-bye.

And every time you lose
a piece of yourself
due to broken love.

And that's what it feels like.

Watching the light go away.
Listening to the sounds
echo
from an empty heart.

People devour people.
While dreams devour
other dreams
and from what remains
anew, *you* rise
like spaceships darting through the sky.
Put this on your life.

No one will ever
quite understand you.

No one will ever
be brave enough to make sense
of all the spinning stars
inside of you.

No one will ever
define you.

Not anyone

but yourself,

and that's what disconnects us,

you and me and them.

No one gets it,
but still,
it is quite comforting knowing,

that at least,
some of us have tried.

FOR COLTON & JEFF

Here's the thing about me.
How I feel about you, us.

I want to see you grow.
I want us to spend our lives together,

reminiscing about our past
and dreaming about our future.

I want to stay with you
in this moment,

to stand beside you
and feel like everything is okay,

like everything that has ever
caused me harm doesn't matter.

Because it doesn't,
not when I'm with you.

I want you, all of you:
Mind, body and soul.

In this life and the next.
To find each other with a smile
and feel the warm welcome of home.

I want to listen to what inspires,
what touches your soul
and what moves you in ways
you'd never imagine.

I want your laughter
the sound of your beating heart
and the slow gentle breeze
you exhale with every breath.

I want your secrets.

The years where you felt most alone
and the ones where you felt invincible.

I want you.

Through good times and bad.
Through violent storms and calm seas.
Through forever
and whatever comes after.

I am yours
and I was,
before I even knew.

Just give me your time,
give me all
of your pieces
and I will promise
to look after you.

I will promise
to set you free.

To carry you
when you don't have enough
to go on.

To fill you
when you feel empty.

I will promise to hold you
when you're coldest.

To give you answers
when your heart is filled
with questions

and to guide you back
where you belong

when you feel lost.

I promise
and I do,

because I choose you
and I want my vows
to comfort you...

to remind you,

that it's you.

It's always has been
and always will be.

I love you

and there will never be another
because

there never was.

I CAN ADMIT THIS

I cried for hours.

I can admit that.

There's no shame
in going through something
that's real.

In dealing with it
and breaking it down
to the atom.

Because there's no shame
in accepting the saddest truths.

No one is invincible.

No one is prone to pain,
to what is meant to hurt.

No one is ever
not affected
by the things they love,
especially when they're gone.

Some people are not meant
to be yours.
Some people are not meant

to be held through the night,
through the day.

Some people are meant
to pass through you,
to fill you
for a few moments,
to just vanish
quicker than they appeared.

And that's bothersome,
you know?

Realizing this
and having to understanding
how to loosen your grip,
how to swallow your pride.

How to accept
when things aren't going
the way you want them to.

And realizing
how some people are meant
to be as free as birds.

Some people aren't meant
to be caged down,
and like the saying goes:

"If you love someone,

let them go and if they return
to you
then they've always been yours."

It's simple, right?

But it's the waiting that devours us.

The space and distance
that manifest themselves
once you've welcomed
the change of things.

And that's what really hurts.

The fact that
there isn't a shelter strong enough
to protect you
from this kind of storm.

The fact that
we are all vulnerable
and too weak
to handle the dealings
of the heart.

So weak,
that some of us live
on our knees
because of it,
because of love

and the sacrifice it brings.

Hell, life is hard,
there is no doubt in that
but loving someone
is even harder.

And realizing this
makes the sun set
but also makes it stop rising.

And broken love,
well,

that is like walking through
a dark path.

You never know
when you'll find the light
and when you do,
you'll have a hard time
remembering what it was like.

Loving the wrong people
can be painful
but in the end,
it is all for something.

It is all
said and done
for a love

that can't be saved

but beautiful enough
to know
that it won't last.

And like all things
that aren't meant to be forever...

all we can do
is reminisce and shed a tear

for a memory
we could have had.

STRONG PEOPLE

People come back stronger,
you know?

So I wouldn't worry much
about how hard you've been hit.

We've all lost a few times
here and there
but it's the way you rise
that counts.

The way you come back
and the way you deal
with what brought you down
to begin with.

That's what makes you
who you are.

How you fall
and how you fly

and how far you extend
your wings—to make sure
you don't ever have to

touch the ground again.

That's what's important here,
remember that.

IT IS NOT FUNNY

You must think it's pretty funny,
giving people advice,

offering them
all types of second chances
when you're just as empty as them.

Telling people
what they're doing wrong,
pointing out their flaws
and scars
and ignoring your very own.

Telling them to forget their past,
what hurts,
when your own wounds
haven't healed.

I get you,
I really do
but the truth hurts, doesn't it?

You want to help everyone
but you barely help yourself.

You want the whole goddamn world
to stop burning.
You want to save everyone

from drowning,
from floating away into oblivion.

Hell, your love is deep.

It truly is,
but what about you?

While you're out saving the world,
who's out saving you?

Who's out telling you
it's going to be okay?

Your arms are extended
but there isn't a soul
out there to hold your hands.

But that's what makes you
beautiful, isn't it?

That's what makes you
a goddamn angel.

You care about others
before yourself
and you love them
before you love yourself.

Because you're on to something.
Something interstellar.

Something holy
and I hope you don't change
for anyone
not even yourself.

Stay selfless.

*It looks so fucking
good on you.*

SOFTEST THINGS

Haven't you had enough?

Haven't you been alone
for far too long?

Are you too afraid of love?

You deserve to be happy.
Life isn't about work,
errands, getting things done,
setting long-term goals,
or making other people happy.

Your life is about you.
About what matters *to you*.

So listen to yourself,
take time for yourself,

to improve and understand
the difference
between what you need,
and what you want.

That should be
your main priority.

Taking care of the little things,

and chasing the moments
that take your breath away.

So maybe you should let
someone love you.

Maybe you should let
someone in.

Maybe you should let
someone look after you
for once,

text you
in the middle of the night
to make sure you're okay.

Call you throughout the day
just to remind you
how much they love you.

Life is hard
but you, my dear,
are made of the softest things,
and you deserve a pair of gentle hands
to lift your head
above the deep waters,

so you could inhale,
and learn to breathe
on your own again.

EVERYTHING IS BROKEN

Now I don't want to
get into it
but there's something about her
that saves me.

Something about the way
she moves her hands
as she speaks,

the way she flicks her hair
toward the backs of her ears.

See,
the thing about her is,

she lets the light in.

She opens me up,
from my broken windows
to the cracked walls
of my soul.

She claims me.

She tells me
I am hers
and there's no fight in me.
No struggling.

No war.
No power
to close the doors
of my beating heart.

Everything is temporary,
all my time is borrowed

and still,
it is hers.

All of me
is hers.

What is here
and what doesn't exist
is hers.

And I'm not the type
to give myself away.

Lord knows
I've given up
on that
many moons ago
but with her,

none of that even matters.

Except the summer
she leaves in my heart

and the winter she rids me of.

I love her
and I do because she embraces me.

And she does so,
so elegantly.

She's patient
and she awaits the storm
and never does she
ever complain about the rain.

Instead,
she holds me
with her arms
and reminds me

why I should never
let her go.

What a beautiful way
to be loved

and

I have no one to thank
other than her.

TO MY BROTHER, HEX

I'm at that point
in my life
where I just want to help people
do some kind of good,
you know?

Because I'm tired
of seeing others
go through the same things
I've gone through,

certain hells
and certain pains

that only the strong
could survive from.

In other words,
if I can save you
from the burning fire,

prevent you
from drowning in the deepest ocean,

I would.

No one should have to go through that,
let alone by themselves.

So there it is.

This is why I am always behind you.

Looking out for you.
Protecting you.

Because I care…

I always have
and I always will.

You are my friend
and I never,
ever,

want to see you fail.

I am your pillar
and I will hold you

everytime

you feel
the need to fall.

BE MORE

Be more
than just words.

More
than just promises.

If you say something,
mean it,
prove it,
make others feel it
and believe it.

As hard as it sounds,
your thoughts define your life
and your life

will always be
a reflection of your thoughts.

So with light
and kindness

do what you feel
because you must,

and do it
for yourself
and not to entertain.

CPSIA information can be obtained
at www.ICGtesting.com
Printed in the USA
LVOW03s1005230318
570816LV00001BB/1/P